Let's know
FESTIVALS
of INDIA

GW00724463

From the Publishers

From the Publishers

Observing the growing interest of people – young as well as old – in religion, culture and history of India and noticing their preference for small books to fit in the steadily diminishing time at their disposal for such reading, we started a new series of coffee-table books, named "Let's Know", and have so far published four such titles. The books have been well-received in India and abroad and have been appreciated for their conciseness, easy-to-read style and wide coverage. We are encouraged to continue the series.

Let's know

FESTIVALS
of INDIA

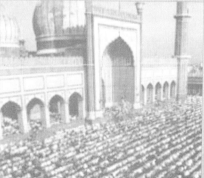

Kartar Singh Bhalla

Kartar Singh Bhalla
Lets know FESTIVALS OF INDIA
Star, New Delhi, 2005

Star Publications, 2005
ISBN 81-7650-165-4

First Edition : 2005
Price : Rs. 225/-
    (in U.K. £ 8.95)

Published in India by
STAR PUBLICATIONS PVT. LTD.
4/5B, Asaf Ali Road, New Delhi-110 002
(E-mail : starpub@vsnl.net)

Overseas Distributors:
INDIAN BOOK SHELF
55, Warren Street, London W1T 5NW (UK)
(E-mail : indbooks@spduk.fsnet.co.uk)

Cover Design, Layout & Photo Typesetting
Jupiter, New Delhi - 110 001, India
E-mail : jupiteradvt@yahoo.com

Printed at Everest Press, Okhla, New Delhi

Contents

Baisakhi

Several Indian festivals coincide with the harvest time and Baisakhi is one of them. Baisakhi, the name derived from the Bikrami month of Baisakh, falls on April 13 every year and on April 14 once every 36 years. Though it is observed almost everywhere in India under different names and with different rituals, it is celebrated with much more enthusiasm in Punjab when the Rabi crop is ready for harvesting.

For Hindus, this day marks the beginning of the solar new year and is celebrated with requisite bathing, partying, and worshipping. It is believed that Goddess *Ganga* descended on earth on this day thousands of years ago, and in her honour Hindus gather along the sacred Ganga River for ritual bath.

Bhangra Dance

Baisakhi has a special meaning for the Sikhs. On this day in 1699, their tenth Guru, Guru Gobind Singh, established the order of the Khalsa , chose five of his followers who volunteered to lay down their lives at his call , proclaimed them *"Panj Pyare"* (five beloved) and gave Sikhs a distinctive personality by prescribing *"Five Kakkas" Kachha, karha, Kesh, Kangha and Kirpan.* On this day, *Melas (*fairs) are held in various towns. Devotees visit Gurudwaras and listen to *Kirtan* (religious hymns) and religious discourses , followed by offerings of sweets to the congregation and partaking of *langar* (community mea)l.

This festival being a harvest festival transcends religious divisions. There is a great deal of merry-making and feasting on this occasion in which people of all shades and beliefs participate. All-night revelries termed *Baisakhi di Raat or Baisakhi da Mela* are held with men dancing the robust *Bhangra* and women the vibrant *Gidda* and all singing folk songs in gay abandon.

Baisakhi heralds the beginning of <u>Naba Barsha</u> (New Year) in Bengal. On 14th April, the people take a ritual bath in the River Ganga or any other nearby river or pool and bedeck their houses with *rangoli* (floral patterns) . In Assam, the *Rongali Bihu*, the Assamese equivalent of Baisakhi, is celebrated on 14 April when the young dress up in their traditional finery and dance the night away. Baishakhi festival is celebrated twice a year in <u>Himachal Pradesh</u> in honour of Goddess Jwalamukhi. This happens in the months of Baishakha (April-May) and *Kartika* (November). In the South, this is the time of celebrating the beginning of Tamil and Telugu New Year. In a ceremonial march, people take out wooden chariots in a procession. On 14 April , Kerala celebrates the new year day called *Vishu* . The celebrations include fireworks, shopping for new clothes and interesting displays called *Vishu Kani.* The people of Bihar celebrate a festival in Vaishakha (April) and Kartika (November) in honour of the Sun God, Surya, at a place called Surajpur-Baragaon.

This day is of great religious import to the Buddhists. Gautam Buddha attained enlightenment under the Mahabodhi tree in the town of Gaya on this day.

Let's know
FESTIVALS *of* INDIA

Basant Panchami

Basant Panchami heralds the advent of spring. It falls on the fifth day of the fortnight of waxing moon (Shukla Paksha) in the Bikrami month of Magha, (January/February). Cool breeze replaces the chilly winds of the winter and there is a touch of fun, frolic and joy in the air. People are heard saying *"Aayee Basant, paala urant"* (In Basant, out winter) .

The day of Basant Panchami is dedicated to Saraswati, the goddess of learning, wisdom, and fine arts since the Vedic and Puranic age. On this day, it is believed, Brahma created Saraswati to dispel the winter gloom and fill the creation with gaiety, music and colours.

Basant Panchmi is celebrated , more or less, all over India but it is observed on a large scale in Punjab and the North when the mustard crop is ripe. The people put on garments in yellow colour, which is the colour of the mustard (*sarson*). They cook yellow rice. The famous folk dance 'Bhangra' glorifies the congregations on this festival. This is a festival of jubilation when the farmers are rich with their yield. Kite-flying is a popular activity of the people on this occasion. In Eastern India, this day is celebrated as Saraswati Puja day when books, musical instruments and paint brushes are worshipped.

Bhangra Dance

Bihu

Bihus are the national festivals of Assam in which all people irrespective of caste, creed and religion participate.. The Assamese celebrate three types of Bihus in a year - *Rongaali Bihu* or '*Bohaag Bihu*', *Kati Bihu* or *Kongaali Bihu* and *Magh Bihu* or *Bhogaali Bihu*'.

Rongaali Bihu is the most important Bihu. It is celebrated over a period of several days. It starts on the last day of the month of *chaitra* which is also the last day of the Hindu calendar year . The day is known as '*Goru Bihu*' on which day cows and bulls are given a ritual bath with the accompanying song "*Lao Kha, Bengena Kha, Bochore Bochore Badhi Ja*. The second day is the main Bihu Day. It marks the beginning of the Hindu new year (mid-April) and advent of spring. It is called Manush Bihu when people greet each other and pay their respect to the elders in the family by presenting them with new '*Gamosa*' (a traditional Assamese hand-woven cotton towel). New clothes are put on, delicacies are prepared in every household for feasting and alms are given to the indigent. Friends and relatives are visited and entertained with food and presents are exchanged. Other main activities during this Bihu are dancing and singing and serving of rice-beer to visitors. Groups of youth go from house to house singing Bihu songs accompanied on the wild and lusty beats of Dhol and Pepa (buffalo hornpipe) which are symbolic of communication of love and romance among the village youth.

Kati Bihu is the most quiet Bihu of the three . Celebrated in the beginning of the *Kati* (7th month of the Assamese calendar - middle of October), it is also called *Kongali* (poor) because there is not much to eat at this time of the year. It is observed by holding silent prayers in the form of lighting of earthen lamps in the paddy fields and near *Tulasi* trees for the success of the crop.

Bhogaali Bihu is celebrated in January, immediately after the traditional paddy crop is harvested. An overnight community function is held in temporary thatched houses , known as *Bhela Ghar* or *Meji Ghar*, specially erected in the barren paddy fields . A Community feast at night near the *Bhela Ghar* is one of the main features of this Bihu. On the following morning the *Bhela Ghar* is lit with fire, culminating the function. There are sports throughout the day. A variety of traditional Assamese sweets and cakes like the *Laru*, *Pitha* etc. are prepared in every home. The next day is spent by visiting relatives and friends to exchange Bihu greetings.

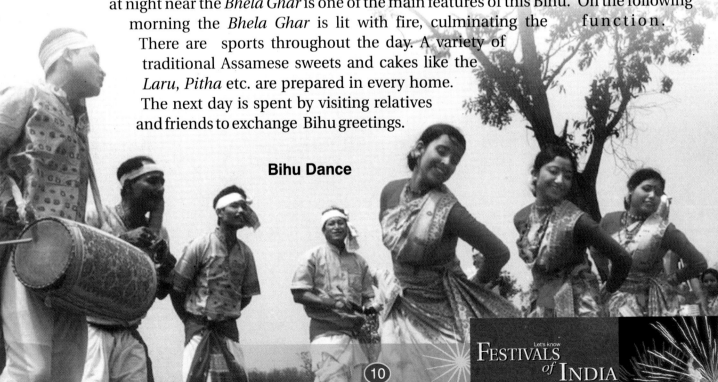

Bihu Dance

FESTIVALS *of* INDIA

Buddha Purnima

Buddh Purnima or Buddha Jayanti which falls on the full moon night in the month of Baisakha (April / May), commemorates the birth anniversary of Lord Buddha, founder of Buddhism. He is believed to be the ninth incarnation of Lord Vishnu. Buddha was born in 563 BC. to King Shuddhodhana and Queen Mayadevi, at Lumbini, Nepal and was named Siddhartha. Before his birth his mother dreamt of a divine light entering her womb. The wise men predicted that the child to be born would be the ruler of the world or a great sage. Gautam Buddha achieved enlightenment and *nirvana* (death) also on the full moon day of Baisakh. It is believed that Yashodara, the Buddha's wife, his charioteer Channa and even his horse Kantaka were also born on the same day. The full moon day in Baisakha is thus celebrated as a thrice blessed day.

Till he was 29, the young prince led a sheltered life in the royal palace of his father . The realization that there was more to life than the lavish and luxurious life he was leading, made him abandon his palace, his wife , his child and all the worldly pleasures and made him embark on search for enlightenment and true meaning of life. After much wandering and searching, Gautama finally attained enlightenment while meditating under a Banyan tree in Bodh Gaya, a small town in Bihar.

For the next 32 years Gautam professed his dharma Buddhism. Henceforth, known as the "Buddha" or "the enlightened one", he began to preach "The Four Noble Truths" to all who would listen. According to this doctrine, people suffer because of their desires and the root cause of all misery is desire. These desires and consequently all problems can be totally eliminated by following the "eightfold path"- right views, right intent, right speech, right conduct, right livelihood, right effort, right mindfulness and right meditation. He died at the age of eighty.

Buddha Purnima is celebrated by followers of Buddhism all over the world. Pilgrims come from all parts of the world to Bodh Gaya to attend the Buddha Purnima celebrations. The day is marked with prayer meets, religious discourses, continuous recitation of Buddhist scriptures, group meditation, processions, worship of the statue of Buddha. The statues of Buddha receive special attention everywhere with people offering them incense, flowers, candles and fruits.

Christmas

Christmas, the birth anniversary of Jesus Christ, is celebrated by Christians with great fervour. It falls on December 25th. It is perhaps the only festival that is celebrated with an equal amount of joy and happiness all across the world. The exact day of the Christ child's birth has never been pinpointed though it is being celebrated since the year 98 AD. In 137 AD the Bishop of Rome ordered the birthday of the Christ Child celebrated as a solemn feast. In 350 AD another Bishop of Rome, Julius I, choose December 25th as the observance of Christmas.

By mid-December, people start decorating their houses, put up Christmas trees, make cribs with figures of baby Jesus, Mother Mary, Joseph. They decorate and illuminate the Christmas tree. Shopping centres become busier as Christmas approaches and often stay open till late.

The celebrations start on 24th evening with carol singing and the Santa Claus visiting houses. The main religious celebration is a mid-night mass followed by the pealing of Church bells to usher in the day of Christmas. On the Christmas day, day services are held in the Churches. The messages and sermons of love and redemption are given out. Christmas cakes and wines are served to visitors and gifts exchanged among friends and relatives.

'Father Christmas' ('Santa Claus') has become the human face of Christmas. Pictures of the old man with long white beard, red coat, and bag of toys are seen everywhere. Children believe that he comes into houses down the chimney at midnight and leaves presents for the children. Father Christmas is based on a real person, St. Nicholas, which explains his other name 'Santa Claus'. He was a Roman Catholic bishop, who lived during the 4th-century in Asia Minor (modern-day Turkey). He was renowned for his munificence to the poor and used to give money to poor people without them knowing about it. It is said that one day, he climbed the roof of a house and dropped a purse of money down the chimney. It landed in the stocking which a girl had put to dry by the fire. This explains the belief that Father Christmas comes down the chimney and places gifts in children's stockings.

Diwali

Diwali (also called Deepavali), the festival of lights, is one of the most important of Hindu festivals. This is celebrated on a nation-wide scale twenty days after Dussehra on *Amavasya* - the 15th day of the dark fortnight of the Hindu month of *Kartika* (October / November). It is believed that on this day Lord Rama returned to Ayodhya after fourteen years of exile and after defeating King Ravana. Deepavali is also celebrated as Naraka Chaturdashi, the day when the demon of darkness and dirt, Narakasura, was destroyed by Lord Krishna. It also marks the day when Mother Goddess is believed to have destroyed a demon called 'Mahishasur'. It celebrates the Victory of good over evil. Another myth links the festival with Lakshmi, the Hindu goddess of wealth and prosperity. The faithful believe that on this day Lakshmi goes around visiting her devotees and sets up residence in the house she finds best spruced up and most hospitable.

Diwali signifies different things to different people across the country. In Gujarat, the festival honours Lakshmi, the goddess of wealth. The Jain community celebrates Diwali as a New Year's Day. Lord Mahavira, the founder of Jainism, is believed to have attained Nirvana on the day of Diwali. For the Gujaratis, Marwaris and business community, Diwali marks the worship of Goddess Lakshmi and the beginning of the new financial year. Sikhs celebrate Diwali to express joy at the return of their sixth Guru, Guru Hargobind, to Amritsar in 1620; Emperor Jahangir had imprisoned him along with 52 Hindu Rajas. The Guru was granted freedom but he refused to leave until the Rajas were also released.

Lakshmi Puja

In Bengal, it is the time to worship Goddess Kali or Durga. In South India, Diwali is associated with Narasimha, the man-lion incarnation of Lord Vishnu. According to a legend, Hiranyakshipu was an evil king. He was unjust and cruel to his people. However, he was almost invincible, having extracted a boon from Lord Brahma that he would be killed neither by beast nor man, neither inside nor outside, neither during the day nor at night. When his atrocities became unbearable, the gods sought Vishnu's help. Assuming his fifth incarnation of Narasimha, Vishnu killed Hiranyakshipu with his claws in the courtyard just before day break, hence steering clear of the boundaries of the boon. For this reason in the south, people light lamps in their houses on the day preceding Diwali.

Dewali is a festival of joy, merry-making, feasting and get-togethers. Gaily-dressed men, women and children go to temples and fairs, visit friends and relatives. Families exchange gifts and sweets. Markets are beautifully decorated. Everybody attired in new and bright clothes captures the social mood at its happiest. This is an occasion for the young and the old, men and women, rich and poor to celebrate. In the evening Laxmi Puja is held and then start celebrations, lighting and fire-works. Houses and business establishments are illuminated with oil lamps, candles and electric lights. Fire-crackers are burst. It is an occasion for spring cleaning and painting of

houses. Numerous people keep the doors and windows of their homes open throughout the night so that Goddess Lakshmi may enter their premises and bring them good fortune. A ritual traditionally associated with Diwali is gambling. Friends get together to indulge in games of chance, dice or cards.

FESTIVALS of INDIA

Durga Puja /Navratri

Goddess Durga

Durga Puja /Navratri commemorates the victory of Goddess Durga over a demon, Mahishasur. who had started torturing innocent people. At the call of the gods, Goddess Durga , astride a lion, fought with the demon and cut off his head.

Navaratri is a joyous Hindu festival which is celebrated during early fall season- from the first to the ninth date of *Ashwin Shukla Paksha* of the Hindu Calendar (late September /early October). The goddess in the form of the Universal Mother is worshiped for nine nights and hence the name *nava-ratri*. On the tenth day, the festival comes to an end with a special *puja* called Vijaya Dasami.

Navaratri festival, which becomes Durga Puja in Bengal and Eastern India towards the latter part, is devoted to Mother Goddess known variously as Durga ; Bhadrakali; Amba or Jagdamba; Annapurna; Sarvamangala; Bhairavi: Chandika ; Lalita; and Bhavani . It marks the universal resurgence of the power of creation over destruction.

Navratri, is celebrated differently in different parts of India. In North India, it is characterized by fasts and solemnity. People read Ramayana during this time. *Ram-Leela*, a stage play of Ramayana ,the story of Lord Rama, is performed during Navratri. It is considered auspicious to start new ventures especially on education and other arts on Vijya Dashami day. It is also common in India to see children start their first music or dance lessons or other educational ventures on Vijaya Dashami.

In Bengal, Durga Pooja is celebrated with boundless fervour and devotion in most households apart from the gaily-decorated *puja mandaps* that are erected in almost every locality. The *puja pandals* have beautifully decorated images of Goddess Durga and community *pujas* are organised. Families visit each other to share feasts and exchange gifts. The festivities start with the first day called *Mahalaya*, when people remember their ancestors (*tarpan*) and *'chakku dan'*, the ritual of drawing the eyes of the image of the goddess, is performed. The first day as well as the following days of *Sashthi, Saptami, Ashtami, Navami and Dashami or Bijoya Dashami* have their own unique rituals. The religious ceremonies start on *Saptami* or the seventh day and are observed till *Dashami*, the tenth day. *'Bodhun'* , the ritual of infusing life to the Goddess, is performed on *Saptami*. On *Sashthi,* mothers keep a fast and pray for the well being of their children. On the 10th day, *Bijoya dashami*, the idols are taken in elaborate processions for immersion in the river or the sea.

In Tamil Nadu, Andhra Pradesh and Karnataka , *pujas* are offered for three days to each of the three goddesses, Durga, Saraswati and Lakshmi and dolls called *Bommai Kolu* are installed and decorated. Gifts of coconuts, clothes and sweets are exchanged. Scenes culled from various stories in the epics and *puranas* are displayed. After the Saraswati puja on the ninth day, the whole set up is taken down on Vijayadashmi. Vijayadashami is an auspicious occasion for children to commence their education in classical dance and music, and to pay homage to their teachers.

In Gujarat and in some parts of Maharashtra and Rajasthan, it is a festival of worship, dance and music. The most fascinating and colourful celebration of Navratri is the *dandiya-raas* and the *garba* . For nine nights, women , decked in finery, dance the *garba* around an earthen lamp or a kalash (pitcher), symbol of divine power. The men sing and dance, clapping their hands in rhythmic movements, or do the *Dandi* dance (stick dance). Beautifully decorated *mandap* are set up for playing *garba & dandiya*. Young men-women wear colourful traditional dresses.

Significantly, no male god is associated with Navaratri. This contrasts strongly with other festivals in which male gods are dominant. Even when goddesses are worshipped in any of the other festivals, they are given this honour as consorts of the male gods to whom the said festival are devoted. But during Navaratri the Mother goddess is not worshipped because she is a consort of some male god. In fact she has no consort (husband). She stands independent, and is worshipped in her own right.

Let's know FESTIVALS *of* INDIA

Dussehra

Dussehra (also known as Vijayadashmi) is a popular Hindu festival celebrated throughout the country with great fervour on the tenth day of bright half of *Ashvina* (September-October). It marks the day of victory of Lord Rama over King Ravana. When Lord Rama was in exile, King Ravana had abducted Rama's wife, Sita. When all efforts failed to recover Sita from Ravana, Rama, alongwith his brother Lakshmana and others, set off for Lanka, killed all the demons and their king Ravana, regained Sita and returned to Ayodhya.

Dussehra festival is a ten-day celebration during which *Ramlila*, a dance-drama narrating the story of Rama's life, is enacted for nine days preceding Dussehra. During this period colourful tableaux depicting various scenes of the Ramayana are taken. On the tenth day, huge effigies of Ravana, his brother Kumbhakarna and son Mehgnatha stuffed with fireworks are raised at various open grounds and set ablaze to celebrate the victory.

Effigies of Ravan

KULU DUSSEHRA : A few days after the country celebrates Dussehra, Kulu, the valley of gods comes alive with an assembly of deities congregating to pay homage to Lord Raghunathji (Rama). The festival in Kullu begins on the last day of Dussehra celebrations elsewhere in the

Kullu Dussehra

country. It lasts a total of seven days. No effigies are burnt. When celebrations are over, a small heap of dried grass is set alight, to symbolize the burning of Lanka and the destruction of the forces of evil. As a final act comes the ceremonial sacrifice of a buffalo. The central piece of the fair is a brightly coloured tent in which the idol of Raghunathji is placed. Then are brought gods and goddesses from all over the valley, some 360 strong, borne on palanquins by priests. After the priests have offered prayers, the idols of gods are placed in a circle around the idol of Raghunathji to pay him homage. Various forms of folk dances grace the festival. While the men wear black berets and tunics of white woollen cloth, the women are attired in rainbow bright *churidar-kurtas*, spangled with silver or gold.

MYSORE DUSSEHRA: In Mysore, Dussehra is a 10-day long royal celebration. While most parts of India celebrate Dussehra in commemoration of Lord Rama's victory over the demon king Ravana, Karnataka celebrates it in honour of Goddess Chamundeswari who killed the demon,

Mysore Dussehra

Mahishasura. Chamundeshwari is the family deity of the royal house of Mysore and during Dussehra her idol is taken in procession in a *howda* wrought in solid gold. Pageants, parades and music create a kaleidoscope of colour and gaiety. On the last day, a colourful procession of soldiers in ceremonial dress, cavalry, infantry, caparisoned elephants and colourful tableaux wend their way from the palace gates to Bani Mantap, where the torchlight parade and a magnificent display of horsemanship mark the grand finale.

Easter

Easter celebrates the resurrection of Jesus Christ after his horrific death by crucifixion. It is the holiest day of the Christian religion. The churches are filled with worshippers, the altars are decorated with flowers, and the music proclaims the joy of the season.

Easter falls on the first Sunday after the first full moon following March 21 - between March 22 and April 25. The date of Easter Sunday was established by the church council of Nicaea in A.D. 325. The celebration of Ester begins six and half weeks before Easter Sunday, with a period known as Lent which lasts for forty days (excluding six Sundays). Lent is a time of fasting and penitence in solemn remembrance of Jesus' suffering and death. It commences from Ash Wednesday sometime in February/March and ends on Holy Saturday, the day before Easter Sunday. The Sunday before Easter is known as Palm Sunday when the church commemorates the triumphal arrival of Jesus in the city of Jerusalem and his welcome by the the entire population, waving palm branches. Maundy Thursday celebrates the last meal of Jesus (known as the Last Supper) with his 12 Apostles, one of whom, Judas, would betray him to the Roman authorities just a few hours later.

The next day, Good Friday (the day of Christ's crucifixion) is a day of prayer and sadness. The following Saturday, Holy Saturday, sees the Church sorrowing, with the same desolate emptiness. And then, at midnight, begins one of the most spectacular of Christian rituals the Easter Vigil. Christians believe that early on Easter Sunday morning, Jesus rose from the dead, proclaiming the triumph of good over evil, and a dark over light. This is ritually symbolized in the mid-night ceremonies: the church is plunged into darkness; one candle is lit, and from it, all the candles in church are slowly lit and a wave of bright lights fills the church; the church bells toll and Christians rejoice that Jesus has come back to life. Once again, light, music and the perfume of incense fill the churches

To symbolize the end of the frugality and abstinence of Lent, on Easter Sunday morning, people offer each other eggs and wear new clothes as a symbol of new life.

Resurrected Christ appearing
before the Marys

Eid-ul-Fitr

'Eid-ul Fitr is observed at the end of the Islamic month of Ramadan. On this day, after a month of fasting, Muslims express their joy and happiness by offering a congregational prayer in the mosques. Special celebration meals are served. Big family groups of relations get together. Children are given sweets, presents and new clothes. They often make offerings to the poor.

The month of Ramadan is one of the five 'pillars' or principals of Islam. Muslims throughout the world celebrate this holy time by abstaining from food during the hours of daylight. When the sun goes down at the end of the day the fast is broken with a meal called the *iftar*. After dinner, it is customary to go out visiting friends and relations. While exceptions are made for the sick, elderly, pregnant and children, Ramadan is a commandment which all healthy adult Muslims are expected to observe.

On the night of the 27th day of Ramadam, Muslims celebrate *Laylat-al-Qadr* or 'Night of Power'. It is said that the Quran was revealed to Prophet Mohammed (pbuh) on this night.

Muslims offering prayer

Eid-ul-Zuha

Eid-ul-Zuha , also called *Bakrid,* is one of the great festivals of Muslims. It falls on the 10th day of the Muslim month of *Dhu al-Hijjah*. It coincides with the Hajj. It is celebrated to commemorate Prophet Ibrahim's (Abraham) readiness to sacrifice his son Isma'il (Ishmael) on the command of Allah. Allah accepted Ibrahim's devotion and obedience and asked him to sacrifice a lamb instead. This is the legend behind the festival. Muslims offer congregational prayer on the day, and afterwards they sacrifice animals to seek the pleasure of Allah. The meat of the animal is shared amongst poor, relatives, neighbours and friends.

Eid Greetings

FESTIVALS *of* INDIA

Ganesh Chaturthi

Ganesh Chaturthi is celebrated as the birthday of Lord Ganesh on the fourth day of the bright fortnight of *Bhadrapada* month of Hindu calendar (September/October). .Ganesh is the god of wisdom as well as of good fortune. He is believed to be the son of Lord Shiva and Goddess Parvati. According to a legend, when Shiva was coming back from his *samadh*i, he didn't know that Ganesha was his son. Ganesha did not let Shiva in the house because mother Parvati was bathing. Shiva got angry and cut his head off and went into the house. When Parvati saw Ganesha dead, she cried and told Shiva that Ganesha was his son. To ease Parvati's grief, Shiva promised to cut off the head of the first living thing he would see and attach it to the Ganesha's body. That creature was an elephant. Ganesha was thus restored to life and rewarded for his courage by being made lord of new beginnings and guardian of entrances. Ganesha is believed to be the destroyer of obstacles–*'Vighna Vinashaka'*; the harbringer of happiness and joy –*'Sukha Kartha'*; the absorber of sorrow and misfortune – *'Dukha Hartha'*; and one who makes wishes come true – *'Siddhi Vinayaka'.* As a granter of boons, Ganesh, the elephant-headed god is propitiated before all other gods and at the start of any new task.

Lord Ganesha

Ganesh Chaturthi is a ten-day festival . Initially a private celebration, it was first turned into a public event by the Indian leader Lokmanya Tilak who used it as a means of uniting people in the freedom struggle against British rule . Though it is observed almost in all parts of India, it is celebrated most enthusiastically in Maharashtra where the *Ganapati Bapa Moriya* refrain is popularly heard throughout the rainy season. The celebrations include discourses, dance dramas, poetry recital, musical concerts, grand feasts, art shows, folk dances and bullock-cart races.

On the commencement of the festival, devotees bring idols of Ganesh to their houses and place them on raised platforms in homes or in elaborately decorated outdoor tents. The priest then invokes life into the idol amidst the chanting of mantras. This ritual is called *pranapratishhtha*. After this the *shhodashopachara* (16 ways of paying tribute) follows. Coconut, jaggery, 21 *modakas* (rice flour preparation), 21 *durva* (trefoil) blades and red flowers are offered. The idol is anointed with red unguent (*rakta chandan*) . Throughout the ceremony, Vedic hymns are chanted.

All through the festival Ganesha is worshipped. Devotees sing and dance ecstatically before the idols of Ganesha. On the 11th day, the image is taken through the streets in a procession accompanied with dancing, singing, to be immersed in a river or the sea . All join in this final procession shouting "Ganapathi Bappa Morya, Purchya Varshi Laukariya" (O father Ganesha, come again early next year).

Let's know
FESTIVALS *of* INDIA

Goa Carnival

The Goa Carnival ('Carnaval' in Portuguese) is the most eagerly awaited and the most enjoyable festival of Goa. The Carnival is exclusive and unique to Goa, and was introduced by the Portuguese, who ruled over Goa for more than five hundred years, during the era of King Momo and has been celebrated since the 18th Century. The carnival is held in February for three days and nights just before the austere 40 days of Lent (period of fasting and penance before Easter). It begins on Sabado Gordo (Fat Saturday) and concludes on Shrove Tuesday (Fat Tuesday) - the eve of Ash Wednesday, which is the first day of the season of Lent.

Although, this festival is primarily celebrated by Christians, it has absorbed Hindu traditional revelry and has turned into a pageantry of sorts. This is the festival of unbridled festivity and merry-making. Colourful processions and lavish floats parade the streets with bands, dances. Grand balls are held in the evenings. It is a carnival of colours, a carnival of fun and a carnival of joy for the people of Goa as well as for the tourists. The carnival concludes with the famous red-and-black dance held by the Clube National in Panijim on the final day.

CARNIVAL

Gurpurabs

Guru Nanak Dev

Anniversaries associated with the births and martyrdoms of Sikh Gurus and historic events connected with the Sikh religion are referred to as *Gurpurabs*. Of these the more important ones are the birthdays of Guru Nanak and Guru Gobind Singh, the martyrdom days of Guru Arjun Dev and Guru Teg Bahadur and the creation of Khalsa. According to Nanakshahi calendar, Gurpurabs are celebrated as follows:-

Guru Sahib Date	Birthdate	Gurgaddi Date	Jyoti Jot
Guru Nanak Dev Ji	1 Vaisakh (14 April)	From birth/praksah	8 Asu (22 Sep)
Guru Angad Dev Ji	5 Vaisakh (18 April)	4 Asu (18 Sep)	3 Vaisakh (l6 April)
Guru Amar Das Ji	9 Jeth (23 May)	3 Vaisakh (16 Apr)	2 Asu (16 Sep)
Guru Ram Das Ji	25 Asu (9 Oct.)	2 Asu (16 Sep)	2 Asu (16 Sep)
Guru ArjanDev Ji	19 Vaisakh (2 May)	2 Asu (16 Sep)	2 Harh (16 June)
Guru HarGobind Ji	21 Harh (5 July)	28 Jeth (11 June)	6 Chet (19 March)
Guru Har Rai Ji	19 Magh (31 Jan.)	1 Chet (14 March)	6 Katik (20 Oct)
Guru Har Krishan Ji	8 Sawan (23 July)	6 Katik (20 Oct)	3 Vaisakh (16 April)
Guru Tegh Bahadur Ji	5 Vaisakh (18 April)	3 Vaisakh (16 Apr)	1 Maghar (24 Nov)
Guru Gobind Singh Ji	23 Poh (5 Jan)	11 Maghar (24 Nov)	7 Katik (21 Oct)
Guru Granth Sahib Ji	17 Bhadon (1 September)	6 Katik (20 October)	Everlasting Guru
Completion of Granth Sahib Ji	1 Bhadon (16 August)		
Creation of the Khalsa	1 Vaisakhi (14 April)		

Going by tradition, the birthday of Guru Nanak is celebrated on Kartik Puranmashi i.e. full moon day of the Bikrami month of Kartik (October/November). The celebrations on all Gurpurabs are generally similar except that the history of each Gurpurab is different.

A couple of weeks before a Gurpurab, *Prabhat Pheris* (early morning processions) begin. The procession goes round a locality singing hymns and collecting offerings. Three days before the Gurpurab, *Akhand Path* continuous and uninterrupted reading of Guru Granth Sahib is star ted in the Gurdwara. It concludes on the day of the Gurpurab. A day before certain Gurpurabs, a public procession (called *nagarkirtan)* is taken out. Sri Guru Granth Sahib ensconced in a palanquin forms the central part of the procession. The route of the *nagarkirtan* is lined with flags, buntings, and floral arches. On the Gurpurab day, religious programme including singing of hymns from Guru Granth Sahib (*Asa-di-var, shabad kirtan*) lectures on the life of Guru Sahib and religious matters are held. After the programme, *Karah Parshad and Langar* (community meal) are served to one and all.

Golden Temple

FESTIVALS *of* INDIA
Let's know

Hola Mohalla

Hola Mohalla is a Sikh festival celebrated in the Bikrami month of Phalguna, a day after Holi, at Anandpur Sahib (Punjab). It was started by the tenth Sikh Guru, Guru Gobind Singh, as a gathering of Sikhs for military exercises and mock battles. It is an occasion for the Sikhs to re-affirm their commitment to Khalsa Panth. During this three-day festival, the *Nihang Singhs* (members of the Sikh army founded by Guru Gobind Singh) carry on the martial traditions with mock battles and displays of swordsmanship and horse riding.

In the general assembly, all religious services are held and tributes paid to Sikh gurus. The function concludes with *Langar* (community meal). On the last day a long procession staring from Takth Keshgarh Sahib passes through important gurdwaras like Qila Anandgarh, Lohgarh Sahib, Mata Jitoji and terminates at the starting point.

Hola Mohalla

Let's know FESTIVALS of INDIA

Holi

Holi is a fun-filled, boisterous and popular festival of India, celebrated on the full moon day of Phalgan of Hindu calendar (March). Holi is a festival of colour. Groups of people men, women and children move from house to house, smear each other with bright coloured powders, known as *Gulal*, throw water-filled balloons at one another and drench each other with coloured waters using long pistons. On this day everybody is in high spirits. It is a day when old grievances and tensions are forgotten. On the eve of Holi, bonfires are set up. Participants walk around the bonfire, pray and invoke the blessings of Agnidev (god of fire).

Holi is an ancient festival. It finds a mention in old Sanskrit literature. There are many legends behind this two-day festival. It is said that Putana, a she-demon, was sent by the cruel king Kamsa to kill the child Krishna. In guise of a beautiful woman, Putana went about in the village of Nandgaon suckling every child to death. But the infant Krishna sucked her breasts till blood started flowing and she succumbed to her death. On the Holi eve, bonfires are lighted to celebrate the victory of Krishna and the death of Putana.

According to another legend, a king named Hiranyakashyapu in his ego ordered his people to worship him as god. His son Prahlad defying his father's orders continued to worship Lord Vishnu and thus infuriated the king. The king asked his sister Holika, who possessed the boon of being immune to fire, to destroy Prahlad. Holika made the young Prahlad sit in her lap and took her seat in a blazing fire with the full conviction that fire could never harm her. But Holika was burnt to ashes and Prahlad walked out of the fire unscathed and alive. The festival is believed to have got its name from this incident and is celebrated by burning effigies of Holika in North India, Uttar Pradesh, Gujarat and Orissa. This also symbolises the victory of good over evil.

In places like Mathura and Vrindawan where Krishna cult flourished and is followed even to-day, this Holi festival is celebrated with great vigour and devotion. Especially famous is the *lathmaar* Holi of Barsana and Nandgaon. Men of Nandagaon (place where Lord Krishna grew up) raid Barsana (place where Radha grew up) with hopes of raising their flag over Shri Radhikaji's temple. The women of Barsana greet them with long wooden sticks. The men are soundly beaten as they attempt to rush through the town to reach Shri Radhikaji's temple.

Lathmaar Holi

In Bengal this festival is known by the name of **Dol Jatra** or **Dol Purnima**. On this day the idol of Mahaprabhu Chaitanya, placed in a palanquin is taken round the main streets and devotees smear Krishna's idol with *gulal*. In Gurudev Tagore's Shanti Niketan, students dress up in saffron-coloured clothes and sing before their teachers and smear them with *gulal*. In Maharashtra Holi is commonly known by the name of "Shimga" and "Rangapanchami". The fisherfolk celebrate it on a large-scale with hilarious singing, dancing and merry-making. In Tamilnadu, Holi is known by three different names- Kamavilas, Kaman Pandigai and Kama-dahanam.

Janmashtami

Janmashtami marks the birthday of Lord Krishna, the eighth incarnation of Lord Vishnu. It falls on the 8th day of the dark half of the Hindu month of *Bhadrapada* (August-September). Krishna, the divine son of Devaki and Vasudeva was born on a stormy night in a prison where his parents had been kept by Kamsa, the wicked king of Mathura. As the legend goes, Kamsa, who was the brother of Devaki, killed all her children at birth because he had been warned that her eighth child would kill him. But on the rainy night when Krishna was born, the doors of the prison opened automatically and Vasudeva, putting the newborn into a basket under blankets, carried him across the Yamuna river, then in spate. Krishna was given to Nand and Yashoda, his foster parents in Gokul, and the newborn daughter of Yashoda, an incarnation of Parvati, was taken to replace Krishna. She was killed by Kamsa.

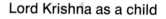

Lord Krishna as a child

Krishna's birth is celebrated in all parts of India with great devotion and enthusiasm. Temples are decorated and illuminated for the occasion. The image of the infant Krishna is bathed at midnight and is placed in a cradle, amidst the blowing of conch shells and the ringing of bells. Devotional songs and dances mark the celebration of this festive occasion. On this day, devotees fast till midnight and they break their fast only after they have rocked an idol of baby Krishna in a flower-bedecked cradle.

Lord Krishna has played many legendary roles during his appearance in the world. He was Arjuna's charioteer. He was a master musician; The music of his flute thrilled the hearts of the *Gopis* and everyone else. He was a cowherd in Brindavan and Gokul. He exhibited miraculous powers even as a child. He killed many demons. He revealed his cosmic form to his mother, Yasoda. He performed the *Rasa Lila*, He taught the supreme Truth of *Yoga*, *Bhakti* and *Vedanta* to Arjuna and Uddhava. He had mastered every one of the sixty-four fine arts. For all these reasons he is regarded as a complete manifestation of God. To the Hindus, he is the supreme statesman, warrior, hero, philosopher, teacher and god himself.

Let's know
FESTIVALS
of INDIA

Karwa Chauth

'Karwa Chauth' is a ritual of fasting observed by married Hindu women seeking the longevity, well-being and prosperity of their husbands. It is popular amongst married women in the northern and western parts of India, especially, Haryana, Punjab, Rajasthan, Uttar Pradesh and Gujarat.

This festival comes 9 days before Diwali on the fourth day of new moon in the month of '*Kartik*' (October/November). Those observing fast get up early in the morning, wear good clothes, eat a little food before sunlight and start the fast. In some sections, Shiva, Parvati and their son Kartikeya are worshipped on this day along with the 10 '*karwas*' (earthen pots) filled with sweets. The fast then starts. Throughout the day no food or water is taken.

In early evening, fasting women dress up in special colourful clothes with *bindis* on their foreheads. Bangles and other jewellery are worn and special henna patterns are applied on the hands. They usually gather together at a common place in the neighbourhood and hear mythological stories underscoring the importance of fast on Karwa Chauth.

After the moon rises, the women see its reflection in water. Then they do *puja* and pray for their husbands' health and long life, and finally break their fast. Husbands pay warm compliments to their wives for undergoing day-long hardship by remaining hungry and thirsty and buy them gifts as a mark of love and appreciation.

Let's know
FESTIVALS
of INDIA

Kumbh Mela

Kumbh Mela (The Pot Fair) is a sacred Hindu pilgrimage and a religious festival where millions of of *sadhus*, pilgrims, and devotees come for historical ritual bathing at four sites on the banks of Rivers Ganga, Yamuna, Saraswati,Godavari and Shipra , considered sacred. Bathing in the sacred rivers is believed to purify and wash of the sins of the pilgrims.

Kumbh Melas are held at various intervals:

Maha Kumbh Mela: This is an extraordinary, once-in-a-life-time festival held at Allahabad , every 144 years.

Purna Kumbh Mela: Takes place after every twelve years and the last one took place in January2001. It is held at the confluence of three rivers Ganga , Yamuna and the mythical river, Saraswati in Allahabad (U.P.)

Ardh Kumbh: Held in the 6th year after Purna Kumbh Mela, i.e. it falls between two Purna Kumbh Melas. It has the same religious value as Purna Kumbh Mela.

Kumbh Mela: This mela is held every three years, rotating through the four cities of Prayag/Allahabad , Nasik (in Maharashtra on the banks of Godavari river), Haridwar (in U.P. where the river Ganga enters the plains from Himalayas) and Ujjain (in Madhya Pradesh on the banks of Shipra river) .

Magh Mela: The Annual Mini Kumbh is held every year except the years of Kumbh Mela and Ardh Kumbh Mela, in the month of Magh (Jan-Feb); hence the name.

The observance of Kumbh Mela is based upon the following legend : Long long ago, gods and demons made a temporary agreement to work together in obtaining *amrita* (the nectar of immortality) from the Milky Ocean, and to share this equally. However, when the Kumbh (pot) containing the *amrita* appeared, the gods, being fearful of what would happen if the demons drank their share of the nectar of immortality, forcibly seized the pot. For twelve days and twelve nights (equivalent to twelve human years) the gods and demons fought in the sky for the possession of this pot of *amrita*. In an endeavor to keep the nectar from falling into the hands of the demons, the gods hid it in four places on the earth, Prayag (Allahabad), Hardwar Ujjain, and Nasik. At each of the hiding places, a drop of immortal nectar spilled from the pot and landed on the earth. These four places are since believed to have acquired mystical power.

Thus, Kumbh mela is observed at these four locations and is attended by millions of people. A ritual bath at a predetermined time and place is the major event of this festival. Other activities include religious discussions, devotional singing, mass feeding of holy men/women and the poor, and religious assemblies where doctrines are debated and standardized. Kumbha Melas are the most sacred of all Hindu pilgrimages.

Kumbh Mela

The 'Kumbh Mela' takes place when the planet Jupiter enters Aquarius and the Sun enters Aries.

Lohri

Like most other festivals in India, Lohri is also related to the harvesting season. It is the culmination of winter. It is celebrated on the 13th day of January in the *Bikrami* month of *Paush*, a day before *Makar Sankranti*. Earlier it was celebrated mainly in Punjab but now in many other parts people celebrate it as a harvest festival under different names.

The focus of Lohri is on the bonfire. On the day of the festival, with the setting of the sun, bonfires are lit . People gather around the rising flames, circle around the bonfire uttering "*Aadar aye diladder jaye*" (May honour come and poverty vanish!), and sing popular folk songs. The munching of seasonal goodies like popcorn, *reori, Gajjak,* jaggery peanuts and sugar cane forms an integral part of the celebrations. Fistfuls of these goodies also find their way into the fire, as an offering to the Sun God. The festival assumes greater significance if there has been a happy event in the family during the elapsed year, like the birth of a child or marriage.

Following the tradition. children go from door to door singing Lohri songs and asking for money for purchase of logs of wood for the bonfire.. They sing in praise of Dulla Bhatti, a legendary Punjabi character (like Robin Hood) who used to rob the rich to help the poor, and once helped a miserable village girl by getting her married off like his own sister. This practice is, however, now gradually dying out.

One of such famous Punjabi songs is:

Holi Bonfire

> *Sunder mundriye..ho*
> *Tera kaun vichara..ho*
> *Dulla Bhatti walla..ho*
> *Dulle dhi viahiyi..ho*
> *Saer Shakkar payi..ho*
> *Kudi da lal pataaka ho*
> *Kudi da saalu paata - ho*
> *Saalu kaun samete..ho*
> *Chacha gaalee dese..ho*
> *Chacha choori kutee..ho*
> *Zamindaran lutee..ho*
> *Zamindara sidaye..ho*
> *Gin-gin paule laaye..ho*
> *Ik pola reh gaya*
> *Sipahi farh ke lei gaya*
> *Aakho mundyo taana*
> *Mukai da dana.. Aana lei ke jana..*

Mahashivratri

The festival of Mahashivratri is universally celebrated by Hindus each year in honour of Lord Shiva (who is known by many names like Shankar, Mahesh, Bholenath, Neelakanth, Shambhu Kailasheshwar, Umanath, Nataraj and others). The 14th day of the dark half of every month is called Shivrati, or "the night of Shiva." Once a year, during the month of *Magha* (February / March), this night is called Mahashivaratri, which means "the great night of Shiva."

There are several stories about the origins of this festival. According to one legend, it was on this day that Shiva first manifested as the *linga* in an effort to break up an argument between Brahma and Vishnu over who was the superior god. In the form of a huge column of fire, Shiva demonstrated his superiority over both of them. Another belief is that on this night, Lord Shiva is said to have performed the *Tandava Nritya* or the dance of primordial creation, preservation and destruction. Still another legend tells of the story of a hunter who, after an unsuccessful day, noticed a pair of deer whom he could kill but he let them off for some time at their appeal. As night fell, fearing predators, the hunter climbed on a tree and in order to keep awake all night, he started plucking leaves from the tree and kept throwing them onto the ground where there was a *Shivlingam* (the phallic iconic representation of Shiva). The following morning, the pair of deer with their offsprings turned up and surrendered them to the hunter but the hunter took pity and let them go. Unknowingly, the hunter had offered his prayers to Lord Shiva by not only showering Him with leaves but also fasting for a day and letting the deer family go. By offering his prayers to Lord Shiva the hunter had gained Lord Shiva's blessings, mercy, compassion and love. Another version traces the origin of the festival to the fact that Lord Shiva saved the entire human race and the universe from destruction by swallowing poison. It is believed that the gods and the demons were churning the Ocean (*Sagarmanthan*) to obtain *amrit* (nectar) to stay immortal. In the process they came across deadly poison that threatened to destroy the entire universe. When the destruction of the universe seemed inevitable, the gods ran for assistance to Lord Shiva, who swallowed the poison without spilling a single drop. That also explains why Lord Shiva's throat is blue in colour for which he is also called *Neel Kanth* A popular belief is that Mahashivratri is actually the celebration to mark the holy union of Lord Shiva and Parvati on this day.

Shiv Lingam

On the day of Mahashivratri, Hindus gather at temples of Lord Shiva, sing *bhajans* (holy songs), offer prayers and recite *shlokas* in honor of Lord Shiva. The Shivlingam is bathed with the five sacred offerings of a cow, called the *panchagavya* - milk, sour milk, urine, butter and dung and offered five foods of immortality - milk, clarified butter, curd, honey and sugar. *Dhatura* and *jati*, though poisonous fruits, are believed to be sacred to Shiva and thus offered to him. Devotees observe fast during the day and offer prayers through out the night and chant the *mantra* "Om Namah Shivaya". Mahashivratri is considered especially auspicious for women. Married women pray for the well being of their husbands and sons, while unmarried women pray for ideal husband like Shiva.

In India, there are twelve "*JYOTIRLINGAS*" of Lord Shiv at twelve places that are sacred to the Hindus. It is believed that all these twelve *Jyotilingas* are "*Swayambhus*" meaning that they sprung up by themselves at these places and afterwards only temples were built. These twelve Jyotirlingas are: (1)Somnath in Kathiawar.(2)Shri-Shailya-Mallikarjun in the South (3) Mahakaleshwar in Ujjain (4) Omkarnath on the bank of river Jamuna (5) Parali-Vaijanath in Marathwada (6) Bhimashanker on the bank of Bhima river (7) Rameshwar in South (8) Naganath in Marathwada (9) Ghrusneshwar at Daulatabad (10) Kashi-Vishveshwar in Benares (11) Kedarnath in Uttar Pradesh (12) Trimbakeshwar in Nasik.

Let's know FESTIVALS *of* INDIA

Mahavir Jayanti

Mahavir Jayanti is celebrated on the 13th day of the bright fortnight of *Chaitra*.(March/April). It marks the birth of Vardhaman Mahavir, the 24th and the last *Tirthankar* of Jains. According to Jain philosophy, all *Tirthankaras* were born as human beings but they had attained a state of perfection or enlightenment through meditation and self realization. They are the Gods of Jain religion. *Tirthankaras* are also known as *Arihants* or *Jinas*.

Mahavir was born into the royal family of King Siddharth and Queen Trishala. After his conception, the wealth, prosperity and influence of the family increased. So his parents named him Vardhaman, the increaser of prosperity. Later, his followers named him Mahavir, the great hero. The two sects of Jains, Digambaras(sky clad) and Shvetambaras (white clad), are divided on the year of Lord Mahavir's birth. According to the Digambar school, Lord Mahavir was born in 615 B.C. The Swetambar school believes that he was born in 599 BC. Both the sects however agree that he was the son of *Siddhartha* and Trisala and born at Vaishali (Bihar). His mother

Lord Mahavir

Trisala is believed to have had a series of miraculous dreams heralding the birth of Mahavir. Digambaras hold that the expectant mother had 16 auspicious dreams before the child was born while the Swetambaras hold that she had 14 dreams. Astrologers interpreting these dreams stated that the child would be either an emperor or a *Teerthankar*.

At the age of thirty, Mahavir renounced the world, adopted the lifestyle in harmony with nature and remained engaged in meditation . He spent the next twelve years in deep silence and meditation to conquer his desires, feelings, and attachments. He also went without food for long periods of time. During this period, his spiritual powers fully developed and, at the age of 42, he realized perfect perception, perfect knowledge, perfect power, and total bliss. This realization is known as *keval-jnan* or the perfect enlightenment.

Lord Mahavira's birth anniversary is celebrated throughout the country but it is celebrated more enthusiastically in Rajasthan and Gujarat, where the Jains are relatively in larger number. Jain Pilgrims congregate at the ancient Jain shrines at Girnar and Palitana in Gujarat and at Mahavirji in Rajasthan. At Vaishali , his birth place, a grand festival known as Vaishali Mahotsava is held .

The idol of Mahavira is given a ceremonial bath called the abhishek and carried in a procession accompanied by bhajan singers and tableaux depicting scenes from the life of Mahavira . Fast is observed by devotees and Jain scriptures are read. Most Jains donate money, clothes and grain to the poor.

Makar Sankranti

The festival of Makar Sankranti coincides with the beginning of the Sun's northward journey (the *UTTARAYAN*) when it enters the sign of *Makar* (the CAPRICORN). It falls on the 14th of January every year according to Solar Calendar. The day and night on Makar Sankranti are exactly of equal hours. This day is looked upon as the most auspicious day by the Hindus. It is believed that the great Bhishma of Mahabharata who had fallen to the arrows of Arjun and who had a boon to choose the time of his death, waited on the bed of arrows to depart from this world only during this period.

Ritual Bathing

Makar Sankranti is also a harvest festival. This festival is celebrated differently in different parts of the country. In Maharashtra , people exchange multi-coloured *tilguds* made from *til* (sesame seeds) and sugar and *til-laddus* made from *til* and jaggery. While exchanging *tilguls* ,people greet each other saying - "*til-gul ghya, god god bola*" (meaning "accept these *tilguls* and speak sweet words"). Married women are given gifts of utensils. In Gujarat, Sankrant is observed in the same manner as in Maharashtra except that here elders give gifts to younger members of the family. In Punjab, the eve of Sankrant is celebrated as "LOHRI". Sweets, sugarcane and rice are offered to the bonfires, around which friends and relatives gather together. The day of Sankrant is celebrated as MAGHI when people sing folk songs , perform folk dances and partake of specially prepared food .In Bundelkhand and Madhya Pradesh the festival of Sankrant is known by the name of "SUKARAT" or "SAKARAT" and is celebrated with great merriment .

In South, Sankrant is known by the name of "PONGAL". It is very popular particularly amongst farmers. Rice and pulses cooked together in ghee and milk are offered to the family deity after the ritual worship. It is a big event for the Tamils and the people of Andhra Pradesh.

The Telugus like to call it 'Pedda Panduga' meaning big festival which continues for four days.In Karnataka, men, women and children attired in colourful tunics visit friends and relatives and exchange pieces of sugarcane, a mixture of fried til, molasses, pieces of dry coconut, peanuts and fried gram. As part of the festival, cows and bulls are given a wash and the horns are painted with bright colours and decorated with garlands, and are taken in a procession to the accompaniment of pipes and drums. In the night a bonfire is lit and the animals are made to jump over the fire.

In Uttar Pradesh, Sankrant is called "KICHERI . It is an occasion to wash off sins with a ritual dip in the holy rivers. At the *Sangam* (Allahabad), Kumbh Mela is held for full one month. In West Bengal every year on this day, a fair, known as Gangasagar Mela, is held when people come from all over India for a ritual dip in the river Hooghly, near Kolkata. In some parts, tribals start their New Year from the day of Sankrant by lighting bonfires, dancing and eating specially prepared dishes sitting together.

Makar Sankranti is a day of kite flying in many parts of India , particularly, Andhra Pradesh, Gujarat, Maharashtra and Madhya Pradesh. In Rajasthan, particularly in Jaipur, skies are filled with kites. In Jodhpur, the Desert Kite festival is held. In Gujarat, appreciating the fervour with which the festival is celebrated, Gujarat Tourism has started hosting an International Kite Festival, which draws experts in kite flying from many states and countries.

Let's know FESTIVALS of INDIA

Milad-ul-Nabi

Milad-ul-Nabi is the birthday celebration of Prophet Mohammed (pbuh) and is celebrated by Muslims as Eid-ul-Milad. Prophet Mohammed (pbuh) was born in Arabia in the city of Mecca on the 12th day of *Rabi-ul-Awwal*, which was Monday the 20th day of April, 571 A.C. Sixty-three (63) years later the Prophet died on the same day. On the day of Milad, the Prophet's teachings are repeated, the Quran is read and religious discourses are conducted in the mosques. The Muslims invite their friends and relatives for a grand feast on this day.

Mohurram

Mohurram is not really a festival. It marks the martyrdom anniversary of Imam Hussein, the grandson of prophet Mohammad (pbuh) who was slain with his family and followers in the battle of Karbala in 680 AD. It is observed in different ways in various parts of India. Devout Shia Muslims all over the world observe a ten - day period of mourning during Mohurram

Islamic history recounts that Imam Hussein with a band of seventy-two came to deliver Iraq from the pretender. They came under siege by the Ommayad army of Yazid and were deprived of food and water for the first ten days of the month. On the tenth day, known as the day of Ashura, Hussein was killed. The story of Hussein's martyrdom is told in parts during the first ten days of the month of Muharram, in gatherings known as majlises where the Shias gather, dressed in black. On the tenth day, in a grand procession, the tragic tale is re-enacted by the mourners who beat themselves and inflict pain on themselves as penance for the heinous crime.

Profusely decorated *taziyas* (bamboo and paper replicas of the martyr's tomb) are carried through city streets. Mourners beat their breasts lamenting and grieving over the murder, crying "Husain! Husain!" This tragedy is remembered with great passion in numerous centres of Shia culture, particularly in Lucknow, Delhi, Agra, Jaipur, Mumbai, Hyderabad. At the end of the day, the *taziyas* are ceremonially buried in the local burial ground known as the Karbala.

Taziya

Let's know
FESTIVALS
of INDIA

Nag Panchami

Nag-Panchami is an all-India festival involving the worship of snakes which is celebrated on the fifth day of the moonlit-fortnight in the month of *Shravan* (July).It is observed in different ways in different parts of India. On this day, some people observe fast . Some worship before the figures of snakes and offer them flowers, fruits, milk, parched rice and parched gram. Lamps are lit and incense burnt before the images. Often people visit the temple of Siva who wears the snake as an ornament. It is believed that the worship will keep them immune from the danger of snake bites .

This ancient festival has many legends connected with it. According to one legend, Lord Krishna once vanquished Kaliya, a huge snake, in the river Yamuna. Later he brought Kaliya to Gokul where the *Gopis* (milk-maids) fed Kaliya with milk and worshipped the snake. It is believed that from then onwards people began to worship snakes as god.

There are many temples and shrines dedicated to snakes. Hardevji temple in Jaipur, Nagathamman temple in chennai and Nagaraja temple at Mannarsala in Kerala are the places where Nag Panchami is observed with great festivity. Adisesha temple at Hyderabad in Andhra Pradesh also celebrates this festival in grand manner.

Snake Charmer

In Maharashtra, Hindu women take an early bath, wear their "*nav-vari*" - nine yards-saree, put on ornaments and offer *puja* to *Nag-Devata*. Snake charmers go from house to house with dormant cobras ensconced in cane baskets, playing tunes on *pungi*, a peculiar wind instrument and asking for alms and clothing. Women offer sweetened milk and cooked rice to the snakes. Cash and old clothes are also given to the snake-charmers. Bowls of milk are also placed at the places which are likely haunts of the snakes.Tourists converge on a little village in south Maharashtra - Battis Shirala near Sangli for this festival. Here the world's largest collection of snakes can be seen.

In Kerala, snake temples are crowded on this day and worship is offered to stone or metal icons of the cosmic serpent Ananta or Shesha. In Punjab Nag-Panchami is known by the name of "Guga-Navami". A huge snake is shaped from dough, which is kneaded from the contribution of flour and butter from every household. The dough-snake , placed in a basket , is taken round the village in a colourful procession in which women and children sing and dance and onlookers shower flowers. The dough -snake is then ceremoniously buried.

Navroze

Navroze is the Parsi New Year which is celebrated on 21st March. The Parsis, the followers of the Zoroastrian, fled from Persia 1200 years ago and migrated to India to escape persecution. They settled down on the Western coast of India mainly Gujarat and Bombay worshipping God according to the teachings of their prophet Zoroaster. The Zoroastrians were called Parsis as they hailed from Pars a province of Persia and are the descendants of Persians. The Parsis are divided into three sects - the Faslis, the Kadims and the Sehensahis.

In the past, Navroze was celebrated for 15 days but now it is observed for only two days. Amongst rituals observed on Navroze day, the most important is spreading of a white cloth on which seven articles beginning with the Persian letter "seen" (the sound) are placed. Another ritual is to grow wheat in earthenware bowls and place them all around the house. The bowls with green stalks of wheat mean the symbol of life and growth. The next day after Navroze the bowls are put in a stream or river . The houses are washed and cleaned and decorated with 'Torans'. Designs like *Rangolis* are drawn. People have early bath and dress up in their best clothes. All types of delicious dishes are prepared and a grand feast is held. A thickish kind of *kheer* called *rava* is prepared out of *sooji*, milk, sugar and cream garnished with roasted dry fruits, sprinkled with rose water. *Falooda , thali* with rose petals, vermillion, rice grains , sprinkler with rose water and coconuts are offered to the visitors. Families attend the Fire Temples where thanksgiving prayers or *Jashan* are offered . It is customary to cover their heads at the Fire Temples. After prayers embracing and greeting of *Sal Mubarak* or New Year greetings are exchanged.

Parsee Temple

Onam

Onam is celebrated after the memory of King Mahabali. It is one festival which is very specific to Malayalees (Kerala). It is a truly secular festival in which people of all religions and castes take part with equal zeal. It occurs during the Malayalee month of *Chingam*, which coincides with *Shravan Masa* of the Indian calendar and it generally falls between August 15th and September 15th. The festivities for Onam last for 10 days

According to the legend, Onam celebrates the golden age of King Mahabali, a mythical ruler of Kerala. Over time, gods became worried as their supremacy was being challenged by the *Asura* king, Mahabali or 'Bali'. They also feared that he would invade heaven. They sought protection from Lord Vishnu and implored him to halt Bali's domination. Lord Vishnu incarnated himself as a dwarf named '*Vamana*'. As King Mahabali was known for his generosity, *Vamana* approached him and asked for as much land as his feet could cover with three steps. The king Mahabali duly agreed, expecting it to be a harmless wish of a poor man.   As soon as he had done so, the dwarf began to grow, and grow, and grow. With the first step, Vishnu covered the sky, blotting out the stars, and with the second, he straddled the netherworld. Realising that Vishnu's third step would destroy the earth, Mahabali offered his head for the last step and thus saved his kingdom.

Boat Race

The Gods were glad, but since Mahabali was so attached to people, he was allowed to return once a year - at Onam.   Onam is thought to be the day when King Mahabali visits his beloved people from the land of exile. This festival is celebrated to welcome the great king Mahabali's return to Earth (Kerala) once every year.

The people prepare for the festival by cleaning their houses and decorating them. On Onam, everybody in the family would be wearing new clothes. Delicious sweetmeats and favourite vegetarian dishes would be cooked and served on banana leaves. One important item that would be visible outside each house is the *pookalam* , a flower mat. This flower mat is like a symbol of welcoming King Mahabali.

During the celebrations there is colourful parade of elephants & fireworks. For entertainment, the popular Indian dance, Kathakali dance would be performed and other spectacular events like carnivals and sports events would be organised. The *Vallamkali* (boat race) is one of the main attractions, and is best seen at Aranmulai and Kottayam. About a hundred oarsmen row huge and graceful boats under scarlet umbrellas to the rhythm of drums and cymbals. In the evening girls perform the Kaikottikkali dance around traditional brass lamps. There is also a fantastic celebration called Pulikali which takes place in Thrissur at the Swaraj Ground, when groups of locals dress like tigers to perform the *pulikali* (tiger dance).

Let's know
FESTIVALS
of INDIA

Pongal

Pongal is an important festival of Tamil Nadu, which is celebrated to mark the withdrawal of the Southeast monsoons as well as the reaping of the harvest. The festival is celebrated for four days . The celebrations start on 13 January and continue for the following three days. 'Bhogi' is celebrated on January 13, 'Pongal' on January 14, 'Mattu Pongal' on January 15, and 'Thiruvalluvar Day' on January 16. This festival is the biggest event of the year for the Tamils as well as for the people of Andhra Pradesh.

The houses are cleaned, painted and decorated. *Kolams* (ground patterns made out of rice flour) are made in the front yards of the houses and new clothes for the whole family are bought to mark the festivities. Even the cattle are gaily caparisoned with beads, bells and flowers. Their horns are painted and capped with gleaming metals.. The poor, the rich, the rural as well as the urban people all celebrate the harvest festival together. A procession is taken out from the Kandaswamy (also spelt as Kandaswami) Temple in Chennai.

Pongal Dance

The first day, *Bhogi-Pongal* is devoted to *Bhogi* or *Indra*, the rain god. The day is linked with the famous mythological tale about Lord Krishna lifting *Gobardhan parbat* on his little finger finger to shelter his people and save them from being washed away by the rains and floods. The day begins with a *til* oil bath and in the evening there is a bonfire made of old cloths, files, mats and rugs.

The second day, *Surya-Pongal*, is dedicated to the Sun (*Surya*). The place where the *Pongal puja* is to be done, usually the courtyard or open terrace, is washed a day prior to the festival, smeared with cowdung, and left to dry. A delicious concoction of rice, moong dal, jaggery and milk is cooked in a new earthenware pot on an open fire. As the *Pongal* boils over and spills out of the pot, children waiting for this go around the pot, clapping their hands and crying *"Pongalo Pongal"*. The excitement of an overflowing pot is considered to be a sure of sign of a prosperous future

Mattu-Pongal, the third day, is the day dedicated to the worship and veneration of cattle (*mattu*). The horns of the cattle are decorated with turmeric and *kumkum*; small bells and flowers are hung around their neck and they are paraded in the streets. The *pongal* that has been offered to the local deities is given to the cattle to eat.

According to a legend, *Pongal* is celebrated because Lord Shiva once asked *Nandi*, his bull, to go to earth and deliver his message to the people - to have an oil bath every day and food once a month. But *Nandi* got it all mixed up when he delivered the message, and told the people that Shiva asked them to have an oil bath once a month and eat every day. Shiva was displeased, and told *Nandi* that since the people would now need to grow more grain, *Nandi* would have to remain on earth and help them plough the fields. *Mattu Pongal* is also called "*Kanu Pongal*", and women pray for the welfare of their brothers. This is similar to the festivals of *Raksha Bandhan* and *Bhai Dooj* celebrated in some states of North India.

The last day is known as *Kanya Pongal*. Coloured balls of the pongal are made and are offered to birds. A kind of bull-fight, called the '*Jallikattu*' is held in Madhurai, Tiruchirapalli and Tanjore in Tamil Nadu and several places in Andhra Pradesh. Bundles containing money are tied to the horns of ferocious bulls, and unarmed villagers try to wrest the bundles from them. Bullock Cart race and cock-fight are also held. In Andhra Pradesh, every household displays its collection of dolls for three days. Community meals are held at night with freshly harvested ingredients. .

Similar festivals are celebrated all over India on the same day, but under different name in each region. However, being a harvest festival, bonfires and feasts are common to all the celebrations of this festival. In Northern India, the festival is known as Lohri while in Assam it is called Bhogali Bihu. In Uttar Pradesh and Bihar it is known as Sankranti, and in Andhra Pradesh it is celebrated as Bhogi, when each household puts on display its collection of dolls.

FESTIVALS of INDIA
Let's know

Pushkar Fair

Pushkar Fair is the most popular and colourful cattle fair held every year on the 11th day of the bright half of the moon (October/November). For 12 days, the little town is taken over by lakhs of animals and visitors.

The Pushkar Lake is also one of the holiest pilgrimage sites in India, the only one in the country associated with Lord Brahma. According to a legend, a king came on a hunting spree to Pushkar from a nearby kingdom. He paused by the waters of the lake to wash himself and quench his thirst. The moment he put his hand into the lake, he was cured of a nasty skin disease. As this news spread, more and more people came to bathe in the lake. They were cured of illnesses, and assured of a place in heaven. Pushkar lake is believed to have been created by lord Brahma himself and has the same sanctity as Manasarover in Tibet. The Pushkar lake is said to take on magical powers during the *Kartik Purnima*, or the full moon during the Kartik month. There are 400 temples and the lake is circled by 52 *Ghats* built over the years by several kings and nobles Till today, people visit the lake on the full moon day of *Kartik* with the hope of attaining salvation. Ancestor worship is also an important aspect of this pilgrimage.

Devotees

The Pushkar Fair is thus a combination of two events happening at the same venue. The Camel Fair, which is the only one of its kind in the entire world, attracts millions of people from rural India along with their camels and cattle for several days of livestock trading. At the same time, the place is a big draw for lakhs of devotees, holy men and sages in various garbs who come to the temple (*Jagat Pita Shri Brahma Mandir*) to pray and take a holy dip in the sacred waters of the Pushkar Lake. The camel and cattle trading is at its peak during the first half of festival period. During the later half, religious activities dominate the scenario.

Camel Fair

The occasion also turns into a great cultural meet. Colourfully dressed sadhus and devotees mingle with musicians, acrobats, folk dancers, traders, comedians, and tourists. The variety of folk dances and songs lend vivid splashes of rhythm and music to the atmosphere that is already charged with excitement of camel races and the cattle fair. Each evening bring different folk dances and music of Rajasthan who perform live shows to the roaring and applauding crowds. The small town of Pushkar is transformed into a spectacular fair ground, as rows of make shift stalls display an entire range of objects of art to daily utility stuff. Decoration items for cattle, camels and women, everything is sold together. Small handicraft stuff is the best bargain for buying souvenirs. The camel and horse races have crowds to cheer. Camel judging competitions are quite popular with animal lovers. This fair attracts people not only from India but also from many other countries.

Raksha Bandhan

Raksha Bandhan (also known as *Raakhi*) is an Indian festival that celebrates the sacred relationship between brother and sister. It is the reaffirmation of a relationship in which a brother pledges to love and protect his sister as long as he lives. The festival is celebrated according to the Hindu calendar on the full moon day in the month of *Shravana*, which occurs sometime in July/August.. Raksha Bandhan is primarily a North Indian festival but is accepted in spirit all over the country though the rituals and customs vary.

Tying Raakhi

Raksha Bandhan is celebrated by a simple ceremony in which a sister ties a *rakhi* which may be a colourful thread, a simple bracelet, or a decorative string around the right wrist of her brother. She applies a *teeka* on his forehead , wishes him long life and gives him something sweet to eat. The brother reciprocates, gives his sister something sweet to eat and hands her a gift in token of love which may be in cash or kind or both.

There are different legends behind the celebration of Raksha Bandhan. *Bhavishya Purana* refers to a battle between gods and demons, and *Indra* (the king of gods) was feeling depressed. At that time *Indra's* wife Sachi took a thread, charged it with sacred m*antras* for protection and tied it on Indra's hand. Indra eventually won the battle and attributed it to the tying of the thread, which he thought was an auspicious act.

Shravan Purnima, as the day on which falls Raksha Bandhan , is considered auspicious by Brahmans. On that day Brahmans change their sacred thread and do *Upa Karma sanskar*. While changing their sacred thread, they re-dedicate themselves to the study of Vedas and persuit of spiritual mission.

In the Mahabharata, Queen Kunti tied *raakhi* on the wrist of Abhimanyu before the *Dharma Yudh* started. In the past, many Rajputs sacrificed their lives to protect their spiritual sisters. Maharani Jodhabai of Mewar sent a *raakhi* to Emperor Humayun and asked for his help. In the same spirit now, girls from schools and women from economically weak sections have started tying *raakhi* to persons in senior positions in public life.

Ramadan

Ramadan is the ninth month of the lunar year of Muslims. God conveyed the message of Quran to Prophet Mohammad (pbuh) through Gabriel in the days of Ramadan. All through the month of Ramadan the devout Muslims observe fast from sunrise to sunset. Purification of the body and soul is the main aim of this observance. The morning "*Sehri*", would generally be cooked in milk, and tea or water. Then the call for prayer is heard from the mosques, and the children and men go to the mosques to offer "*Namaz*". Women stay at their houses and recite the Quran.

But the fasting during the days of Ramadan does not affect the daily routine of the Muslims and they go on with their daily chores. As the sun sets, the call for the *Maghrib* prayers is heard from the mosques and the fast is broken. It is called "*Iftar*". The fast is broken sipping water and eating a few dates and some fruits. The food eaten as *Iftar* is called *Iftari* and special delicacies like fried cornflower, boiled grams and lentils, meat *kebabs* and sweet meats are taken. Thus the month of Ramadan passes and the sighting of the new moon brings glad tidings of Eid-ul-fitr and the end of the month of Ramadan .

While, lying, slander, denouncing others behind their back, bearing false witness or coveting someone else's possessions are forbidden to Muslims even in normal times, these acts during Ramadan are considered particularly abhorrent as they would undo all the good gained by fasting.

Let's know
FESTIVALS
of INDIA

Rama Navami

The festival of Ram Navami marks the birthday of Lord Rama, who is believed to be an incarnation of Lord Vishnu. According to the Hindu calendar, it falls on the ninth day of the *Chaitra* month (March). Rama, the eldest son of King Dashratha, was banished to the forest for 14 years at the instance of his stepmother who wanted to see her own son Bharata ascend the throne in place of the elder brother Rama. In these 14 years of exile, Rama waged and won a war against Ravana, the King of Lanka, who had kidnapped his wife Sita. Rama returned to Ayodhya after triumph over Ravana and after completion of the period of banishment and ascended the throne. As he started ruling, he was forced to banish his wife from the kingdom, following a villager's adverse comment about her association with Ravana.

Lord Rama, wife Sita, brother Laxman and devotee Hanuman

Rama is believed to have been sent in the world to destroy evil and uphold righteousness. He embodied the highest ideals of man and is called the *Maryada Pushottam*, which means the perfect man. Rama was the ideal son, an ideal ruler. an ideal husband and an ideal brother. *Ramrajya* (the reign of Rama) has become synonymous with a period of peace and prosperity.

Ram Navami commemorates the noble ideals for which Lord Rama stood. Swami Vivekananda, one of the foremost harbingers of national renaissance said: "Wherever four Hindus live, Rama and Sita will be there".

Ram Navami celebrations begin with a prayer to the Sun early in the morning . (Rama's dynasty is believed to have descended from the Sun and is called *Raghuvansh* or *Raghukul*). Devotees observe fast on the day. Temples are decorated and the image of Lord Rama is richly adorned. The holy Ramayana is read in the temples. Rath yatras or chariot processions of Ram and his wife Sita, brother Lakshman and devotee Hanuman, are taken out from many temples. Hanuman is worshipped for his unflinching devotion to Lord Ram and his worship forms an important part of the Rama Navami celebrations

Ayodhya, the birthplace of Lord Ram, is the focus of great pomp and celebrations. A huge fair is organized there for two days. In South India the '*Sri Ram Navmi Utsavam*' is celebrated for nine days with great fervor and devotion. Those talented in the art of story telling narrate the thrilling episodes of the Ramayana. The *Kirtanists* chant the holy Name of Rama and celebrate the wedding of Rama with Sita on this day. It is an extremely colourful ceremony, highly inspiring and instructive. In Andhra Pradesh, this festival is celebrated with great religious zeal, particularly the Ramnavami festival at Bhadrachalam, which is celebrated for ten days from '*Caitra Suddha Saptami*' to '*Bahula Padyami*' (March/April). The *Kalyanotsavam* (wedding of Rama and Sita) celebrations attract about three lakh devotees every year. It is a day of festivity for *Ramabhaktas*.

Rath Yatra

Jagannath Rath Yatra (known as the Car Festival to western world) is one of the most spectacular festivals of Hindus celebrated in the coastal town of Puri (Orissa) in July - on the second day of bright fortnight of the Hindu month of *Asadh*. It celebrates the annual visit of Lord Jagannath (by which name Lord Krishna is known in Orissa) to his birthplace , *Gundicha Mandir*, outside the city. Lakhs of people converge at Puri for this festival. Images of Lord Jagannath, his brother Balabhadra, and sister Subhadra, are taken in giant wooden chariots to *Gundicha Ghar*. The deities are kept there for a week and then returned to the temple. The journey back consists of another ritual, known as *Phera Rath Yatra*.

Each deity has its own massive chariot, which is replica of the temple. Jagannatha's chariot, *Nandighosha*, is yellow in colour, 45 ft high and has 16 wheels, each one seven feet in diameter. About 4,200 devotees draw the chariot. Balabhadra's chariot , called *Taladhvaja*, is blue in colour and has 14 wheels. Subhadra's chariot is the smallest, with 12 wheels and is called *Deviratha*. The festival has been celebrated since ancient times. According to a legend about its origin, Jagannatha is said to have expressed his desire to visit his birthplace every year for a week. Accordingly, the deities are taken to the *Gundicha Mandir* every year. According to another

Rath Yatra

legend, Subhadra wanted to visit Dwarka, her parent's home, and her brothers took her there on this day. The Yatra is believed to be a commemoration of that visit. According to the *Bhagavad Purana*, it is believed that it was on this day that Krishna and Balarama went to Mathura to participate in a wrestling competition, at Kansa's invitation.

On the day of the *yatra*, people get up early and offer prayers to Jagannatha. The chariots are lined up in front of the Puri temple. Devotees offer prayers to the deities. Descendants of the Maharaja, heralded by gaily-caparisoned elephants, sweep the chariot platforms with a gold-handled broom and sprinkle scented water. All buildings are colourfully decorated with flags, buntings and awnings of bright colours. Women in colourful saries crowd the balconies. Men and women rush to pull the chariots along the main street. The Lord who is rarely glimpsed outside his inner sanctum, is on this day easily accessible to everyone in the streets of Puri .

Devotees

Children are seen on the streets carrying miniature versions of the chariots with tiny idols installed on them. Shops and houses are decorated with flowers, lights and *rangoli*. Most people refrain from eating non-vegetarian food. Nowhere else is a deity, once installed and consecrated, taken out of the temple. The Jagannatha Temple at Puri is the sole exception to this general rule. In fact during the Ratha Yatra, the chariots become mobile temples, which sanctify the city.